Copyright © 2021 by Glynnette Byrom Scott
Illustrated by Kristy Wells
Edited by Stephanie Carter

All rights reserved. This book or any portion thereof may not be reproduced or used in any manner whatsoever without the express written permission of the publisher or copyright owner except for the use of brief quotations in a book review.

Printed in the United States of America

THE DAY I MARCHED WITH MARTIN: A DAY TO REMEMBER/ GLYNNETTE BYROM SCOTT – 1st Edition

First Printing, December 2021

ISBN 978-1-7353141-9-8

This book is published by:
STePH Publishing, LLC
Waldorf, Maryland
www.stephpublishing.com

The Day I Marched With Martin

A Day to Remember

By Glynnette Byrom Scott

Illustrated by Kristy Wells

This book is dedicated to:

the two men who made this book possible,
my dad, Julius Byron and my former Pastor,
Rev. Dr. Michael E. Haynes,
my mother, Margaret Byron,
my brother, Oliver Byron,
my husband, Richard Scott,
and to all who encouraged me to share this
memory with others and to you, the reader.

The Day I Marched With Martin

A Day to Remember

When I was just a little girl, before I was old enough to go to school, I learned about a very special man named Dr. Martin Luther King, Jr.

My Dad often spoke about Martin Luther King, Jr. He would explain to me and my sister, Beverly, what it was like to be "colored" living in what was referred to as the "South", the southern part of the United States. "Colored" was a word used to describe people who had brown skin like mine. We now use words like "Black" or "African-American".

I knew Dr. King was a special man because he taught non-violence, and because he was brave, loving, and kind. He wanted Black people to have the same rights as white people. Dr. King battled long and hard, but he didn't use weapons or his fists. He used powerful speeches. His speeches helped change laws to make America a better place for everyone.

Dr. Martin Luther King, Jr. traveled all over the Southern United States to make change. He traveled to the Northern states, too. In April 1965, I was eleven years old and in the sixth grade when Dr. King made a special visit to my hometown, Boston, Massachusetts.

Boston was a special place to him. He lived there when he was a graduate student at Boston University. Boston is also where he met his wife, Coretta.

While Dr. Martin Luther King, Jr. was living in Boston, he attended my former church, Twelfth Baptist Church, now located in Roxbury, Massachusetts. My former pastor and Massachusetts State representative, Reverend Michael E. Haynes and Dr. King were lifelong friends.

On April 22, 1965, Dr. King spoke to the Massachusetts Legislature, the group of the lawmakers for my state. He was invited to speak there and the lawmakers, also called legislators, gave him a special award.

The next day, on April 23, 1965, Dr. King led a march to protest "de facto segregation" in Boston. De facto segregation happens when people are separated by color by society, not by law.

My dad always respected Martin Luther King, Jr. for all the work he did, and he liked the way he spoke to bring about change. So, when my dad heard that Martin Luther King, Jr. was coming to Boston, he decided to go to the march and to take my sister and me along with him. I was so excited! I never dreamed that I would march with the incredible man I had heard so much about.

But not everyone in my family was excited. My mother, who had grown up in the South, did not want to go to the march because she thought there might be trouble. Sometimes there was trouble where Martin Luther King, Jr. spoke or marched because some white people did not like what he was trying to do.

Sometimes the demonstrators and marchers were beaten, spit on, hosed down with fire hoses, attacked by police dogs, arrested, and taken to jail. Although she was a little afraid, I'm glad that my mother did not object to my dad taking us to the march. She knew he would not let anything bad happen to her precious daughters. She let us go with him.

The night before the march, I couldn't sleep. I remember tossing and turning in my bed all night long. I got up a few times and tiptoed into the kitchen to see what time it was. I remember being disappointed that there were still several hours before morning. I was so impatient for dawn to come, but I finally dozed off to awaken to signs of daylight peeking through the wooden venetian blinds and pink frilly curtains in my bedroom.

April 23, 1965 had arrived. That morning, my sister and I got up without our parents calling us. It turned out to be a cloudy, damp, chilly day with rain threatening, but we didn't care. We were both so excited about the day's big event. We could hardly wait to leave the house. We washed up quickly and put on our "marching clothes". We called them "marching clothes" because we were wearing them to march with Dr. Martin Luther King, Jr.

I wore my navy-blue cotton pants with a long-sleeved white jersey decorated with tiny pink and yellow flowers. I took my freshly polished white sneakers from the closet and hurriedly put them on. My sister wore her khaki-colored cotton pants with a long-sleeved pale pink jersey and, of course, her freshly polished white sneakers. We now felt and looked like we were ready to march.

My mother fixed one of our favorite breakfasts, Cream of Wheat. My sister and I ate the Cream of Wheat quickly. We grabbed our coats before our mother kissed us all good-bye. We scurried downstairs and out the front door. We climbed into our bronze colored Ninety-Eight model Oldsmobile with Dad at the steering wheel and off we went. We were finally on our way to Carter Playground where the march was to begin.

March Instructions

THIS IS A NONVIOLENT DEMONSTRATION, therefore,

1. You are expected to refrain from any hostile act or word, even when provoked.
2. The march will be quiet, orderly and serious.
3. You are expected to follow the instructions of trained marshals who are easily identified and stationed at regular intervals in the march. Marshals will remove any inappropriate signs.
4. At the Common, follow the lead of your marshal. There are several reserved sections--one for the aged and handicapped (please tell your marshal if you need a pass for this section), one for honored guests, and one for a group of marchers who, under marshals' directions, will leave the main line of march and return to the Common later. IT IS IMPERATIVE THAT MARCHERS FOLLOW THE DIRECTIONS OF THE MARSHALS IN KEEPING THE AISLES CLEAR.
5. At the Common, lunches should be eaten before the rally begins. All sandwich wrappers and papers should be deposited in the bags which the marshals will carry through the crowd.

GENERAL INFORMATION

Dr. King will start the march; then it is planned that he will leave the march with community leaders to meet with the Mayor and School Committee. He will rejoin us at the Common.

The marshals will direct one section of the march past City Hall and the School Committee. This section will return to the Common before the rally begins.

An offering will be received during the rally. If you plan to give a large donation, please inform you marshal so that he can have it acknowledged by the platform.

Portable toilets, medical coverage, water supply, and lunches are available. Please check with you marshal.

The march committee has worked closely with Superintendent Mulloney and others of the Boston Police Department, who have cooperated fully in the arrangement of this march.

Carter Playground was in the South End section of Boston. Because of the crowd, my dad parked several blocks away and we had to walk. As we approached Carter Playground, we saw a lot of people, some were black, and some were white. Everyone received a program with instructions, and we were told to line up for the march, side by side, in rows.

We finally lined up. A teenaged white boy who looked a couple of years older than me was on my right. He had dark, curly brown hair and soft, brown eyes. My sister and my dad were on my left. We waited a short while and then the march started. Our arms were hooked at the elbows, shoulder to shoulder. In the middle of the rows and rows of people was Dr. Martin Luther King, Jr. This was his march, and I was there with him!

FREEDOM SONGS

THIS LITTLE LIGHT OF MINE

This little light of mine,
   I'm going to let it shine.
This little light of mine,
   I'm going to let it shine.
This little light of mine,
   I'm going to let it shine,
  Let it shine, let it shine, let it shine.

1. Everywhere I go, I'm going to, etc.
2. Up in Massachusetts, I'm going to, etc.
3. Round the School Committee, I'm going to, etc.
4. Down on my knees, I'm going to, etc.
5. We've got the light of Freedom, we're going, etc.

WHICH SIDE ARE YOU ON

Which side are you on, boys, which side are you on?
Everybody which side are you on, boys, which side are you on?

My mother was a freedom fighter and I'm her son, you bet.
   Will you fight de facto or Tom for Ross Barnett?

Come all you Freedom fighters, lift your voices and sing.
   Will you follow Louise Day Hicks or Martin Luther King?

WOKE UP THIS MORNING

Woke up this morning with my mind
   Stayed on Freedom
Woke up this morning with my mind
   Stayed on Freedom
Woke up this morning with my mind
   Stayed on Freedom
Hallelu, Hallelu, Hallelu.

1. Singing and praying with my mind, etc.
2. Walking and talking with my mind, etc.
3. Bussing to school with my mind, etc.
4. Casting my vote with my mind, etc.
5. Woke up this morning with my mind, etc.

OH FREEDOM

Oh Freedom, Oh Freedom, Oh Freedom over me
And before I'll be a slave,
   I'll be buried in my grave
And go home to my Lord and be free.

1. No more weeping...
2. No segregation...
3. No more sadness...
4. No de facto
5. Oh Freedom

WE SHALL OVERCOME

We shall overcome, we shall overcome
   We shall overcome, some day.
Deep in my heart, I do believe
We shall overcome some day.

1. We are not afraid...today
2. The truth will make us free,...some day
3. We'll walk hand in hand...today
4. Black and white together...today
5. We are not alone,...today
6. We shall overcome...someday.

I was thrilled as we slowly began to walk up Columbus Avenue. We walked past the many shops, business offices, and brick apartment buildings that lined the street. As we marched, we sang the songs of the Civil Rights Movement that I had heard many times on TV and on the radio. Songs like, "Oh Freedom", "This Little Light of Mine", "Woke Up This Morning", "Which Side Are You On," and one of my favorite songs that still brings tears to my eyes, "We Shall Overcome". When we were ready to sing, "We Shall Overcome", we crossed our arms, right over left, just as the demonstrators had done so many times in the South. I was so proud! Proud to be Black, proud to be marching, and proud of Dr. Martin Luther King, Jr.

The march ended at the Boston Common Bandstand in downtown Boston. There Dr. Martin Luther King, Jr. gave a speech. We could see him at the podium, and we could hear every word he said. He took his time delivering his message, in a deep voice, slowly and clearly, to the people of Boston. He spoke against racial segregation in housing, employment, and de facto segregation in the school system. He encouraged the people of Boston to pursue brotherhood for all saying that the time is now.

APRIL 23
FOR
MARTIN LUTHER KING
AND
BOSTON

I didn't know that on that day history was being made. The march in Boston was the only march led by Dr. King in the Northeast. I had no idea that just three years later this man who stood so strong would be shot down and assassinated because of the hatred that lies in the hearts of some people.

I will never forget the day I marched with Dr. Martin Luther King, Jr. It is forever carved into my memory just like a sculptor carves his stone. I will never forget the songs we sang as we walked along Columbus Avenue. I will never forget the proud feeling I had. I will never forget Dr. Martin Luther King, Jr., and the important role he played in America's history.

Glossary of Terms

Non-violence - the use of peaceful means, not force, to bring about political or social change

State Representative - a person elected by a district within a state to be a member of the state Legislature

Legislature - a body of persons having the power to make laws

Legislator - a person who makes laws; a member of a legislative body

Segregation - the action or state of setting someone or something apart from other people or things or being set apart

De Facto Segregation - is the separation of groups that happens because of fact, circumstances, or customs

Civil Rights Movement - a mass protest by African Americans in the mid-1950s to late 1960s to achieve Civil Rights equal to those of whites, including equal opportunity in employment, housing, and education, as well as the right to vote, the right of equal access to public facilities, and the right to be free of racial discrimination

Assassinated – the murder of prominent person in a surprise attack for political or religious reasons

Sculptor - an artist who makes carvings of stone or wood or by casting metal or plaster

Reference: https://legal-dictionary.thefreedictionary.com